Spiritual Espionage
Going Undercover for the Kingdom of God

Edie Bayer

ISBN: **978-0615985510**

DEDICATED

To my Husband, Darryl, without whom this
book may never have been written. You exemplify
the very nature of Jesus with your selfless love.

CONTENTS

The Lord had spoken to me multiple times about finishing up this book and getting it printed. However, as much as I wanted to, it just wasn't a priority.

Until God made it one.

We were hosting Darren Canning, and as I was setting up the book table with Darren's books and my husband's CD's, I heard the Lord say, "Your book needs to be on this table." I knew then it was a priority for God.

Even then it took me a year to get it finished.

It's the small things that count with God. I can have the best intentions, but without actually obeying and doing what I have been told, it means nothing. It doesn't count. There are no brownie points for "I meant to!"

The Lord has wanted me to get this book into print and to get it in the hands of believers – YOU -- to motivate and bring you to action. It is not necessarily BIG actions that bring change. Rather, it is small acts of obedience that manifest radical change in yours and other people's lives.

God is no respecter of persons. If He can use me – and He does – He can use you, too! But you have to say "Yes"…. and then actually take the steps to move out and do it.

God has his own training field for each of us. Even if we are in the same ministry setting as others, the same church, or even the same FAMILY, by design we all have unique experiences with God.

He is waiting to have yours with YOU.

So, Step OUT, Step UP, and do what the Lord God has called you to do. Today. Now. In obedience.

I pray and hope that my small act of obedience in sitting down to finish this book will have the chosen effect - to motivate you to do what you hear the Lord telling you to do.

All Blessing, All Honor and All Glory to God!!

Edie Bayer

EDIE BAYER

.

1 PROMOTION REQUIRES OBEDIENCE

I was driving along in November of 2011, shortly after I resigned my position at Joan Hunter Ministries, when the Lord spoke to me. I was meditating on my time there. I was thinking that I would like to have a ministry like Joan's, a global ministry and all that entails.

The Lord interrupted my thoughts.

"Are you ready to go to the next level?"

Without thinking, immediately I said "YES! Anything you want me to do, Lord!"

He said, "Alright, but you cannot tell me NO."

As many sermons as I have heard on this particular subject, I should have known better! A few days later, the Lord spoke to me again. He said, "I want you to go to the Methodist Church on Sunday."

I was stunned. If I am anything at all, I am a Charismatic Christian. I raise my hands in church, dance, sing and shout out, "Hallelujah!" and "Amen!" This would be torture!

Immediately, my knee-jerk reaction was to say "Never!!" But I remembered what the Lord said, that I CANNOT tell Him "No".

I gulped and answered, "Alright Lord."

The next day, I was trying to weasel out of going to the Methodist Church. I said, "For how long, Lord?"

He said, "You don't know for how long. A day, a week, a month or the rest of your life." Again, I said, "Alright Lord."

That night, I told my husband what the Lord had told me --- that my assignment was to go to the Methodist Church. He was shocked, and was not sure that I had heard from God at all! However, after I filled him in on the few details I had, and my conversation with God about going to the next level, my husband reminded me of a story I had told him about a time when the Lord had asked me to go and sit in the parking lot of the Methodist Church — this *same* Methodist church!

At that time, I was head usher at the local Cowboy Church. I had to get to church early to unlock the doors and start to set up for the services and get things in order for the other ushers and for Pastor to arrive. The Lord, knowing the schedule I was on, and the timing of the services at the Methodist Church, asked me to stop and sit in the parking lot of the Methodist Church to pray for the people there for five minutes.

I did, feeling foolish at the time, and I asked God "What am I supposed to pray about for FIVE MINUTES?"

It's funny now, but back then in my earliest of early ministry days it seemed like an insanely long period of time to pray for someone that I didn't even know, never mind an entire church! Since then, of course, I have prayed for literally thousands of people that I have never met and many, many more in the ministry and church services that I have worked in with Joan Hunter and Paulette Reed. How small we think!

That day, I crept into the parking lot of the Methodist Church slowly, trying to be unobtrusive hoping no one would see me, and parked at the end of the row so I could escape quickly if I needed to (if someone noticed me praying for them, or asked me what I was doing there!)

I will never forget it. I shut the engine off, which immediately brought silence into the cab of my pickup truck. I looked around, but there was no one in the parking lot. I started to pray, slowly at first, hesitantly, not really knowing how to pray or even about what.

Instead of praying for just five minutes, I ended up praying for them in the parking lot for fifteen minutes, weeping and praying in tongues. It was amazing how the time simply flew by! I couldn't believe it. I was amazed! But I did it. I prayed for a people I had never known, for the very first time.

As I drove out of their parking lot that day, changed inside, I wiped my tear-streaked cheeks. Feeling foolish once again --- this time for doubting God --- I continued to Cowboy Church.

I had already told my husband what I believed that God wanted me to do as my assignment. I believed that He wanted me to try to convert the Methodists to Evangelical, Holy-Roller, Bible Thumping Charismatic Christians (like me!) a task for which I was completely unequipped. I cried on his shoulder, out of frustration and maybe even a little fear.

I didn't WANT to go to the Methodist Church!

My husband comforted me as best he could, but he couldn't make my date with destiny at Methodist Church go away! Only God could, and I couldn't tell Him "No".

That night my husband had a dream that I was a warrior with a huge sword, that I had been given this monumental assignment from God. In his dream, I was talking to God, and told Him that I wanted a horse. The Lord told me to strike the ground with my Sword, and a

3

white horse appeared. He said that the horse had a large chest and I had large breasts! Of course, in Christian dream interpretation large breasts are not sexual, but have other meanings depending on the context of the dream.

In this particular dream, the large chest speaks of a large heart to nurture and to comfort. The horse's chest meant strength and ability (picture any hero with a large chest), authority and power — *horsepower*, if you will.

Upon waking, my husband relayed this dream to me, and said that he felt that it was a sign from God. He also stated his unwavering commitment to this new assignment. He was in agreement, and backed me 100%.

I had his blessing.

2 REMEMBER YOUR INSTRUCTIONS

Finally, Sunday morning came, and I resigned myself to a bleak, religious experience – and not a good one.

God still had not told me what I was supposed to do. He hadn't given me any details. I knew there was no way that He would want me to just sit in a pew. As I was getting ready to go, walking into the closet, I asked Him, "Lord, what do you want me to do there? What is my assignment?"

The Lord quickly responded, "I want you to walk the halls, pray and intercede and take back ground for the Kingdom that the enemy has stolen!"

I was so relieved!! Pray? That was EASY! That I know how to do!

Next, He told me, "I want you to tell the Pastor that you are there on an assignment from God. Tell him that I have heard his cries, and answered his pleas. I am sending help. It begins with you. There will be many others behind you, that he should expect them." Again, He said, "I am sending help."

The Lord went on to tell me EVERY detail of my upcoming experience. He told me to leave at exactly 10:30, so that I would have 15-minutes before the service to walk the halls and pray. (Remember the story of the FIVE minutes? FIFTEEN MINUTES this time! Same church.)

He said that they would send someone to help me when I arrive; that I was to walk the halls and pray according to Ezekiel 37, and breathe new life into their bones according to His word.

He also said that there would be "some of like spirit" that would recognize me and would be attracted to me, but that my job was to discern devils, and that I would know them because they would be staring at me. He said that they would know me immediately, that the devils would discern me at once, and recognize the invasion.

God wanted Heaven to invade earth, and He was using ME to do it!

I felt much relieved and at ease, other than giving the Pastor a prophetic word, which I was a little nervous about.

Regardless, I dressed conservatively, according to the direction of the Lord, in black slacks and a blue and black shirt, with a camisole underneath, and a simple gold chain with no ornamentation – nothing at all to draw attention to myself God said.

I realized at the moment that God gave me those precise instructions on how NOT to draw attention to myself that God wanted me to *go undercover*! Spiritual Espionage for the Kingdom of God!

Now, instead of being anxious and nervous about the pending visit to the Methodist church, I was excited and enthralled at the mission ahead of me. Like an engrossing novel, I couldn't wait to see how it turned out!

As instructed by the Lord, I left my house at 10:29 and waited at the end of my driveway for the clock to turn to 10:30. I knew the service began at 11:00am, and that it wouldn't take more than 15 minutes to get there from my house. I arrived a little before 10:45, and got out of my truck. I grabbed my bible, and headed inside, excited to see what would happen. I followed a man inside the building, one who was wearing an old fedora. I wondered if HE was a devil!

Once inside, the long hall from the side entrance I had come in had framed, hand drawn pictures of people on the walls. I continued on into the main foyer where tables had been set up in a semi-circle with literature set out on them. I circled the room from table to table, glancing at the literature that had been set out for people to read. I continued on my circuit, quietly praying in tongues under my breath.

I noticed a table with a sign for the "Angel Tree" in front of it. I recognized this ministry name, as it was Christmas time – the second Sunday of Advent, the Christian New Year.

Even though I am a seasoned Christian, I had just learned about Advent from a woman at the church I had attended the previous Sunday, so God was starting to make it all come together for me. I continued on down the hallway on the other side of the foyer, still praying quietly for the breath to come from the East, the West, the North and the South. There was a beautiful young woman with a handicapped child in a stroller in front of me in the hallway. She smiled brightly and asked me, "Can I help you?"

I realized immediately that God's battle plan was unfolding. I hadn't been in the building more than a minute or two!

I said, "Yes. This is my first time here."

I found out her name was Linda, and the little handicapped girl was Heather. I was told the little girl was not her child, and Linda informed me that she worked with the youth at the church. She said that she would be happy to take me on a tour, but that she had Heather and couldn't do it herself.

She was so genuinely pleasant, and I knew that God had sent her to help me, "a like Spirit." This was getting more exciting by the minute.

There was a long hall in front of me, and I asked Linda, "What's down there?" She recognized one of the other children's church associates, called to her, and asked her to give me a tour. How awesome is our God? He had sent me to walk the halls, and had provided the means to do so --- with a tour guide!

This lady was visibly not excited about doing it, but agreed nonetheless. She walked me into the children's building, and promptly passed me off to her husband, Jim.

He was very agreeable, and took me around the entire building, showing me every bible study room, every part of their hallway network....and I prayed, and I nodded and smiled, and I prayed, silently and under my breath in tongues, I prayed!

Finally, we wound up at the main foyer again, where he walked me straight up to the senior Pastor, who was standing at the entryway to the sanctuary in his flowing Methodist-minister gowns. He was surrounded by a group of men, elders and deacons I assumed.

One of them at the Pastor's left elbow introduced himself, and said that they usually have two services on Sundays, but one day during the year, during Advent, they hold a joint service with all of the congregation in attendance.

I couldn't believe it! God had sent me to this church, on the ONE DAY out of the year that every single member was present!

I said, "What timing!" He gave me a quizzical look, and I said quickly, "God's timing is perfect!" What better time to be able to decapitate spirits than when all the bodies are in the house of the Lord?

After that Jim marched right up to the Pastor with me in tow and introduced me. I took a breath, and said, "I am here on assignment from God."

The Pastor looked at me a little funny for a second, then laughed and said, "Of course you are!"

I looked him square in the eye, and said, "No. REALLY. I am here on assignment from God."

The same deacon at his left elbow laughed loudly, and said, "Wow, that's GREAT! *What a great line!* I'm going to use that when I visit other churches!"

One of the other men at the door took me by the elbow and steered me into the sanctuary, then called his wife over to take me to sit with her so I had no opportunity to deliver the Word that God had given me, which didn't really matter because I had forgotten about it! I was so overwhelmed by everything that had already transpired, I had completely forgotten about the Word I needed to deliver to the Pastor.

I excused myself from sitting with the elbow-steering-man's wife by telling her that Linda had asked me earlier in the morning to come and sit with her during the service. Entering the sanctuary, I looked for her where she said she would be. To my astonishment, she was in the VERY FRONT PEW! One couldn't get any closer to the altar than where she sat.

I walked up to her, rather taken aback, and laughingly I said, "I didn't know you would be in the VERY FRONT!"

She explained that her daughter was lighting the candles that morning, so she would not be able to sit with me. She asked another member of her children's church team to sit with me a few rows back in the children's section, so I would not be alone during the service.

I told her that I didn't know the procedures, and would she mind showing me? She smiled, and said, "No problem!" This gracious lady mentored me through the rituals as the service progressed, not judgingly, but with love. I really liked her. How awesome is our God! He sat me with someone He knew would show me the ropes patiently, the same as she would show a child, as a teacher.

I looked around the room, knowing that since everything else that the Lord had said had so far come to pass, that my job at this point was to discern devils.

I was astounded to find people in the choir staring at me -- two men in their light blue choir robes. THE CHOIR! They were not staring menacingly, but definitely had their spiritual antennae up. I realized that God again was totally correct. A little later in the service, I saw a woman staring at me, who quickly turned away once she caught my eye. One other time a woman walking down the aisle after communion stared at me. I was breathless. The Lord had not told me what to do after I discerned the devils, so I prayed for the people housing them.

The Pastor brought the Word, communion was served and the whole time the gracious teacher on my right showed me when to stand, when to sit, and how to fulfill the communion obligation.

A little later we were dismissed. I exited the sanctuary, not looking for the Pastor, but finding him anyway. He was standing at the same door as on the way in. He shook my hand warmly, and said he hoped I would come back. I didn't even think about the Word that the Lord had given me for him.

I left the building, and realized when I was part of the way home, praising God for this new "assignment", that I had not given the Pastor the Prophetic Word from the Lord. I felt bad because I thought I had missed the mark.

I told my husband all about the meeting when I saw him, and Darryl was enthusiastic and supportive. He told me how proud he was of me for taking on this monumental task, for being so totally in tune with the Lord and what He is doing now.

I was effusive, and bubbling over with the Joy of the Lord. It's incredible when the Lord uses you for His purposes.

I also told him I wanted to send a thank-you note to the Pastor of this church, telling him how wonderful the hospitality was, and include a copy of Darryl's new soaking CD, "Soaking Reign".

Darryl and I have a joint ministry, called Kingdom Promoters and I wanted to include an invitation to this Pastor to have Darryl play at the church. I felt the Lord say that He would write the letter! How much better could it get?

I did finally deliver the Word the Lord had given me. Only it was in written form, and not face-to-face verbally. I included the Word in the thank you letter, along with Darryl's CD.

I still am not sure if God intended me to deliver it verbally or in writing, but some things we'll just have to ask Daddy when we get home.

The Lord had already told me my next assignment for the following Sunday....The Presbyterian Church.

EDIE BAYER

3 BE BOLD

I had no sense of forboding or anxiety as the Lord told me my next assignment was the Presbyterian Church. There was no nervousness, just excitement! I was being used of the Lord!

I was striking the ground with my Sword and making things happen!

On Sunday morning the Lord told me again how to dress, right down to my shoes. He said, "I want you to dress more conservatively than the Presbyterians!" Again, He stated, "Do not draw attention to yourself."

He also told me, "They will not trust you."

So, the only question I had for the Lord was about timing. The Presbyterian Church was tiny, very elegant and quaint. It was the very typical beautiful white chapel complete with chiming bell tower and red doors. The Lord told me to leave only 10-minutes before service.

I said, "Lord the church is so tiny!"

He said, "It won't take as long to walk the halls then, will it?"

Of course, again He was right.

When I entered the building directly behind two other ladies, in the main foyer was a woman who was talking to an older man and stacking papers.

This woman asked, "How are you?"

I answered, "Fine, how are you?"

She smiled politely, waiting for me to say something else.

I continued, "It's my first time here."

She responded, "Welcome!" She then turned and went right back to her stack of papers.

That was it. No offer of hospitality, no tour. I was on my own.

I walked into the sanctuary and sat down at the very back of the building, in the last pew. I was only in my seat for a moment when I thought, "This isn't why God sent me here!"

Standing up, I went back into the front foyer. I had to work to get the woman's attention this time, saying "Excuse me, Ma'am" a couple of times. She finally drew away from her important work of stacking papers to look at me.

I pointed to the hallway at the other end of the Sanctuary. "What is back there?"

The Lord was right again! She didn't trust me. Suspiciously she peered at me and said, slowly, cautiously, "Offices… The fellowship hall… The kitchen. Choir room." Then she added, almost as an afterthought, "The restrooms."

I smiled the biggest smile I could, and asked, "Is it ok if go take a peek? It's my first time here, and I would just like to poke around."

Again, suspiciously she squinted at me through her glasses but after a few seconds nodded. She went back to her paper stack.

I headed to the back of the sanctuary, praying silently, making my way around two women, one on a walker and one using a cane. I passed the kitchen, and some classrooms. It was a short walk. I turned the corner, and almost ran into the man in front of me in flowing black robes. He surprised me.

"Oh, good morning!" I said, a little flustered. "Are you the Pastor?"

He smiled graciously and answered, "I am the visiting minister, Dale. And you are?"

I said, "Edie Bayer. It's my first time here." He was very pleasant, but deliberately blocked my path. He wanted me out of that part of the church, so he asked another woman passing by to take me into the sanctuary.

Her name was Sue, and she took me under her wing. She was very affable, offered coffee, and asked me to sit with her. I said I would be delighted.

Church small talk ensued. She told me all about the history of the church but how they have no permanent pastor right now. Dale, the visiting minister, she said, was a Hospice Chaplain. Soon she was distracted by a someone she knew, and I was free to look around the room.

There were several visitors that morning. The two ladies that I followed into the building were visitors and were seated immediately behind me, with two more visitors seated directly in front of me. It must have been the visitors section, with us purposely hedged in by congregants.

Suddenly, I heard the Lord say, "Take the first fish that comes up!"

I thought about it for a second, and quickly realized that a fish is a soul, and a soul is a person. I knew that He was sending someone, and I was to help that person in whatever way the Lord had in mind.

Deliberately, I started "fishing", talking to those around me, and those that came up to meet me. I soon learned that one of the two women I had followed in was Scottish, so we had common ground.

15

She had a haunted look in her eyes, a gaunt face, and it was obvious that she was hiding some huge hurts. I felt that she was the "fish" that the Lord wanted. I prayed for her silently.

Minister Dale preached from a death perspective about death, something he knew all too well as a Hospice Chaplain. His stories were engaging and it was obvious that he had loved the people that had been in his care, all of whom had died. He made them come alive in his message, and I felt that I had met them personally. He was an impressive speaker.

Eventually it was time for the usual "meet and greet". I turned to the woman with the haunted eyes and asked her some questions, to try to get a handle on what was going on in her life. I found out her name was Teresa, and her child was getting married. She was checking out the church as a possible place for the wedding, since she was from the Woodlands.

I said to her that I wanted to speak to her after the service. She hesitated, but agreed, stating she didn't understand why I wanted to talk to her. I simply wanted to pray for her.

At the end of the service, I turned to her again, but the church lady in charge of weddings beat me to her. I said I would pray for her, and she looked relieved and said thank you. I told her I still wanted to speak with her, and she asked me "What did you want to talk to me about?"

I said, "I want to pray with you."

She said, "Is that all?"

The world has been taught to believe that prayer is NOTHING, just words, and that nothing ever comes from it. The Bible says that the fervent, effective prayer of a righteous man availeth much.

I KNOW God hears me! His Word tells me so, and I choose to

believe the Bible.

Is that ALL, I thought at the time. Isn't that the BEST?

Of course, I didn't say that. I said, "Yes, I want to pray with you."

She gave me her email address after declining Facebook. She asked me for my cell phone. I got her email address, and she went to speak with the church lady.

I thanked Sue for her hospitality, put on my coat, and headed for the door.

For the second time that day I almost physically ran into Minister Dale. He was standing at the door, smiling enthusiastically and holding out his hand.

The Hospice Chaplain had told some stories about people that he had met and become friends with in his duties as chaplain during the message, and I knew that there had to be many more.

I grasped his hand in both of mine, and said, "You are an Author!"

He smiled politely and started shaking his head to say "No".

I felt the heat rise on my chest, and started to prophesy over him.

I said, "Oh yes, you are! You are an author. There is a book inside of you that needs to be written. Now write it!"

I said it forcefully. I think I even poked him in the chest with my finger as I spoke! The look on his face was worth every minute of time that I had spent in the church that day. It was priceless.

It was obvious that he had been inquiring of God, "Should I write the book?"

His jaw dropped, obviously stunned. He got his answer that morning.

Once I was outside the building and headed for my pickup truck the tears came, slowly at first, then a fountain of sobs erupted from somewhere deep inside of me, in the privacy of my vehicle.

I was weeping, at first I didn't know why, maybe relief, maybe joy, but I began praying for the one fish that the Lord had sent to me, Teresa. I prayed for the trauma that had attached itself to her, for the huge hurts that had inflicted such pain into her life, so much pain that it poured out her eyes.

I resolved to email her as soon as I got home.

I couldn't wait to tell my husband all about this second assignment, all the details, and everything that transpired. We were on the couch, chatting later that night, when the Lord dropped on me my next assignment....the Bible Church.

He also told me that my assignments are "tied into" my husband. I did not know what that meant, but I was sure He will clarify! (*Author's Note: I think I have it figured out now!)

I did email Teresa. To date I haven't received a response. I still pray for her every day, and look for an email from her.

4 MULTIPLICATION MIRACLES

Have you ever experienced a TRUE Miracle of Multiplication? I have! Here is what happened.

New Year's 2012 Miracle Manifestion.

I went grocery shopping on New Year's Eve for dinner and for the following day. Having finished, I was in line at HEB, checking out. I had had a long grocery list, and on it was tortilla chips to munch and to watch movies as a family.

I had picked up a bag of "Tia Rosa" Megathin tortilla chips. You've seen them, in the brown bag. I finished grocery shopping and put all my groceries on the checkout stand conveyer belt, just like normal.

I went into my wallet to get my debit card out, and glanced at the sacker bagging my bags of groceries. I noticed TWO BAGS of tortilla chips.

I thought, "Well, maybe I DID pick up two bags....". But I KNEW I hadn't. I then turned to look at the checker briefly, a young man, college age or maybe a senior in high school.

I looked back at the bags of groceries a moment later, and now there were not just two, but THREE BAGS of Tortilla chips!!

At this point, the sacker, who was extremely friendly -- a perfect angel one might say -- asked me the normal HEB questions, "Did you find everything ok?" and "Would you like help out to your car?"

In a state of shock and yet somehow still trying to act "normal", I said, "No, I have a truck, I'll be fine."

He looked at me, and said, "Really, I don't mind."

The way he said it made me stop and stare at him. Frankly, I was still so stunned by the loaves and fishes tortilla chips that had just multiplied right AT THE CHECKOUT COUNTER in front of dozens of people that I hadn't really paid any particular notice to him before then, other than how friendly and helpful he was, and REALLY joyful.

Looking back at it, I wish I had taken him up on his offer of help out to my truck. I would have loved to hear what he had to say about the chips multiplying on the checkout counter. I had never seen him or the checker before at HEB, so I concluded they had to be in cahoots, that the two of them HAD to be angels!

I pushed the cart as fast as I could out to my truck to look at my grocery receipt. Of course the truck was sandwiched in between two vehicles. I squeezed my cart in between my truck and a mini-van in which two elderly people were sitting, the woman driving and the man in the passenger seat. She was eating a hamburger.

I thought, "that's Odd…the woman is driving." But then brushed it off.

I had to push the cart right up next to her door, and it would have been impossible for her to get out. I leaned over to speak to her through her window.

Smiling, I said, "I hope you aren't going to want to get out any time soon!"

She made a pleasant squinty face, waved me on, and took another bite of her hamburger.

I stood for a moment, scanning my grocery receipt, to see how many bags of tortilla chips were on there.

Just as I had suspected, only ONE. I KNEW that God had multiplied those bags of chips!!!

I finished loading my groceries into the cab of my truck, still stunned and in awe at this literal miracle manifestation of multiplication that had just occurred. I turned, after I closed my door, and the woman looked right at me, and mouthed "Happy New Year!"

She had the biggest smile I have ever seen.

I pushed my cart into the buggy catcher and turned back to get into my truck. I waved at this elderly couple. The old man waved back. I didn't see if she did or not.

By now I was on another planet, in another universe completely, flying high because God had just showed up in person, and manifested two bags of tortilla chips!! In hind sight, I am sure the old couple were angels, since I've NEVER seen an old person smile that huge.

Driving home, I thought, "I would LOVE to see the security camera tape of that transaction! Did God's hand actually come and put the bags of chips on the counter? Did the bags of chips clone like a cell dividing? Didn't ANYONE see it??? How did they show up and no one noticed it?"

Then of course, the doubt set in, and my thoughts switched to "There had to be two bags of chips left behind by the person in front of me...the checker put them on the counter there, because they were a three for one special....maybe I DID pick up three bags of Tia Rosa

Megathin Tortilla chips???"

But I KNEW in my heart that God had multiplied those chips at the checkout stand.

When I got home, I couldn't wait to tell Bobb, my son the legalistic teenager. I had prayed and asked the Lord how to tell him, since as of the date of this writing he was not walking with Jesus. His future is certain, however, since his destiny is as a Daniel, a David, and a Gideon.

I handed him the receipt, and said, "Do me a favor, and see how many bags of chips are on there."

I left the room, and when I returned, all he said was "One."

I then proceeded to tell him the entire story of the bags of chips multiplying on the checkout counter. He looked at me straight in the face, very dead-pan, and said, "So, you walked out of HEB with two bags of tortilla chips you didn't pay for."

I laughed!

I said, "They were a gift from God!!"

He then said, "Obviously they were already there, someone else had paid for them and left them behind." Brilliant minds think alike, eh?

I grabbed two bags of the Tia Rosa Megathin tortilla chips in the brown paper sack, held them up in front of him, and said, "Right, Bobb. How many hundreds of brands of Tortilla Chips are there in the world, that someone directly in front of ME in line should buy two bags of exactly the same tortilla chip that I am buying and leave them behind on the counter???"

That silenced him. Even a legalistic teenager knows everyone eats Doritos. He did not seem convinced, but I know another God-Seed was planted in him.

Next was Darryl. I expected him to hoop-and-holler "HOORAY!" and shout out, "Hallelujah, Praise the Lord!"

This was his very first miracle of multiplication, however, and he looked at me askew in disbelief. His face said, "Either you are putting me on, or you are totally crazy!"

I could tell he was trying to believe (Lord, help me with my unbelief!), but he had the same thought process as both me and Bobb…how many bags of chips were on the receipt, someone had obviously left them behind, I must have picked up the extra bags.

Finally, he said, "Are you SURE God multiplied the tortilla chips? TORTILLA CHIPS???"

Of course, by now I was totally certain. When I was alone in the room with God, I asked Him.

I said, "God, I am grateful that you showed up and multiplied the tortilla chips, honest, I am. I have heard of loaves and fishes multiplication before, but have never actually seen it happen. But God…. why did you multiply TORTILLA CHIPS?"

His answer came immediately. It was amazingly clear, distinctive, and to the point.

He said, "Well, think about it!"

THINK ABOUT IT? Not the answer I expected. Not a booming, thunderous voice from the clouds saying, "IAM who IAM…" I didn't even get an explanation of why He hadn't chosen manna, ice cream or even whole wheat bread.

Think about Tortilla Chips?

So, that is EXACTLY what I did. For the next 5 days I thought about tortilla chips. I researched in the bible and online. In hindsight I am sure God laughed at me. I read the bag of Tia Rosa Megathin Tortilla Chips over and over, thinking there was a clue on there somewhere. Maybe Auntie Rosa had something to do with it. I read about the Tia Rosa tortilla chip company and what the ingredients are in tortilla chips.

I looked up tortilla chips online, and was actually surprised to find out that they originated in Los Angeles in the 1940's, and not in Mexico as I had always thought. I looked up corn, how to grow it, what it means in the Bible and in dream interpretation. I contemplated that Mexico missions might be in my immediate future, after all, Tia Rosa, Mexico....

I thought about Tortilla Chips for 5-days straight.

Finally, I went to God with my thoughts. I had NONE.

I said, "God, I have absolutely no idea why you would choose tortilla chips. Will you help me? Why did you multiply the tortilla chips?"

His response, again, was short and to the point.

He said, "How do I feed the masses?"

I was shell shocked...ANOTHER RIDDLE!!! Once again, discouraged and still no answer.

I immediately went to Darryl, who by now was fully convinced of our own personal multiplication miracle after listening to me talk about God multiplying the tortilla chips for five days straight.

I told him what God had said. I then asked him, "How does God feed the masses?"

Darryl said, "With Manna."

I said, "Right, but in the Bible, He uses bread...."

Darryl said, "And wine, at Cana."

I said, "Yes, right. However, at every miracle feeding, He uses bread."

Darryl laughed at me. Smiling, he said, "Of course He does. What are tortillas?"

THEN the light bulb came on, and I understood! Bread. Fed to masses. Mexican bread. Flour tortillas, and corn also, but bread nonetheless.

Again, I went back to God, and thanked Him not only for the multiplication, but for the answer to my questions, as well.

He said, "All my puzzles are that easy."

I beg to differ!

Now, please understand! I have studied dream interpretation, have countless dreams written down, multiple journals, several dream-book encyclopedias by different authors and notebooks full of dreams stacked by my bed….none of these puzzles are easy!

Using dream interpretation as my foundation I was looking for some deep, complicated answer…not something simple like flour tortillas as bread.

The Lord also spoke to me that had I lived in Ezekiel's time with their understanding that solving those riddles would be just as easy as flour tortillas.

Lastly He told me, "The season of Multiplication has begun."

That is a VERY GOOD WORD.

5 THE ANOINTING

The Lord spoke to me about the Bible Church, "This might take a little longer, a couple of weekends."

I understood a few things about the Bible Church. I understood there is a stronghold of religiosity there. I had heard that they do not believe that healing is for today, that it stopped 2000 years ago when the disciples died, that when they died supernatural healing died with them.

Of course, I have seen many multiple miraculous healings during the time I worked with Joan Hunter's healing ministry, and have been miraculously healed of a couple things myself.

I know for a fact that healing IS for today, and I am living proof!

With that understanding I knew in advance a couple of the spirits that the Lord wanted me to fight....deception and affliction.

The Lord instructed me that I could wear my "normal" clothes, blue jeans and nice shirts, just like always. What a relief!! Of course, I didn't realize that I would blend right in with all the others at this church. God always knows!!

I immediately went into the ladies bathroom when I got there. Inside I met Terri while we were both washing our hands, a very pleasant early 50's lady with long hair. I informed her that it was my first time at the church. She smiled, and said, "That's nice. Welcome."

I tried to pry more out of her, but she directed me to the information booth. She did say that they have classes after the service, and that hers was cancelled because the teacher was out of town. I figured I would stay for a class, too, since I was already there.

I went to the information booth, after walking the halls and praying in tongues and in the natural for the people and the building. It was becoming very comfortable now, and very normal for me. There was no opposition to me at any part of the walk.

I sat in the sanctuary, and awaited the service. It was very normal, but quiet! No hand clapping, only two worship songs.

The preacher came up and introduced the special guest speaker, an evangelist from Uganda, a Presbyterian minister. His wife and children came up and did an African song and dance about Jesus. It was cute, but stilted. The African minister was better, he was evangelistic and preached long and strong about getting out of one's seat and ministering to those who were lost.

How ironic, I thought, that this man was preaching to the deceived about saving the lost.

After the service, I started for the upstairs classrooms.

On the second or third stair, God spoke to me, saying, "You know you are free to leave."

I stopped in my tracks, and asked Him, "Lord, do you WANT me to stay, or do you WANT me to go?"

He responded, "Stay."

So I continued upstairs. I chose a class about money and teenagers. I figured it couldn't hurt, as I was in the throes of financial issues with my teenage boy about buying him a car, wanting him to get a job, teaching him to drive, and talking about responsibility.

I was amazed. The class answered an astounding number of my questions, and helped me set out a track to run on with my son. I was totally blown away by God! He set me up!

At the end of the class I ran up to the speaker, and thanked him for the information. He was surprised and happy. I told him it was a divine appointment and that God had sent me there because of the things going on in my son's financial circumstances. He was thrilled that someone enjoyed the class.

Interestingly enough, the Pastor and his wife had sat behind me during this class.

The following weekend, I went to a conference given by Paulette Reed and Barbie Breathitt on Saturday. Barbie interpreted a dream of mine, wherein I was a passenger in a car driven by a dark-headed woman, who was going around a curve too fast to the right, and went off the cliff. She interpreted it to mean that I needed to ask God who the person is that was going too fast and missed the turn. As a passenger, it was beyond my control. The convertible meant either open revelation, or no covering. She said this person was not listening to God's voice, and was going to miss it. I came home convinced that it was my husband. He's dark headed….!

On Sunday, I again went to the Bible Church. I arrived a little later than the weekend before. However, I was still able to make a circuit of the building, bind, cast out devils and loose the Holy Spirit into the place. I prayed for the air in the building. I prayed for the building. I prayed for the people. I prayed against the spirit of deception, and that revival would come to the Bible Church.

The message was great. I found out the Pastor could really preach! The previous week the Pastor had mentioned that the church had a "growing problem", and no wonder their attendance was growing! His message was wonderful, and he really knew the Word.

During the middle of the service, the Lord spoke, and told me that I had completed my assignment, and He was proud of me. He said that I am His prophetic arrow, pulled from His quiver, and shot straight to the hearts of His people.

It was wonderful to hear the voice of the Lord!!

However, it was still too quiet in that sanctuary for my tastes. There was no hand clapping, no hollering, no AMEN and HALLELUJAH shouts coming from the congregation. I missed my Pentecostal, Charismatic Christian brethren!

Regardless, I moved on after the service to the class. I was anticipating another amazing class. I made another circuit of the building praying, before I went upstairs.

Sadly, the anointing was gone. The Lord had told me the assignment was completed. I didn't ask if I should stay for the class, I just assumed that I should. In hindsight, I knew it was an error.

The class was short and disinteresting. The Pastor wasn't in the room as he was the week before. I was ready to go as soon as the speaker stopped speaking, but someone asked a question and he talked for another 10-minutes. It was terrible, and as soon as he dismissed us, I almost ran from the room and down the stairs.

Suddenly I was completely aware of the alien surroundings, felt totally out of place, and I couldn't wait to leave.

When your assignment is over you will know it. The anointing will be gone. What once was easy will be hard. The doors that used to fly open will no longer be available without force, and in some cases, will not open at all no matter what.

God deliberately gives us His grace, the Anointing, to perform the tasks that we cannot complete without Him.

6 NOW GO

My final act of obedience in this series of small acts of obedience, although I didn't know it at the time, was to attend a Catholic church in the Woodlands for a few weeks.

A full month, the Lord said.

I was so discouraged! I DEFINITELY did not want to attend the Catholic Church!

Darryl gave me an encouraging word and said that I might find some Charismatic Catholics in there. I tried to look at the positive side with him, but it wasn't easy for me. The Catholic Church symbolized the epitome of religious dogma to me.

It is very difficult for me to hide in the Catholic Church. I don't know the routine, the stand-up-and-then-sit-down-now-kneel portion of their services, or the traditions. I've only attended a few Catholic services, and those were when Darryl was playing his trumpet.

However, I agreed to go where God sends me. That's the deal.

I got a bulletin from the church, to keep as EVIDENCE that I actually sat in a Catholic church – just in case somebody didn't believe me!

My first trip to the Catholic Church in the Woodlands was intense. I arrived early and sat in the parking lot, praying. I saw lots of expensive cars and lots of people in expensive clothes headed into the giant brick and glass-fronted building.

I noticed that the Catholic women were not terribly shy about their bodies. They didn't cover up much. I was really surprised. I always thought of Catholics as oppressed and extremely conservative.

Hollywood.

I discerned spirits – lots of them. I made my way across the parking lot and entered the building. There was a line at the entrance, and I couldn't understand the hold-up but I waited in line with everybody else.

Once I got further into the hallway, I realized that a few feet and several people in front of me there was a little stainless steel dish attached to the side of the building. It looked a lot like a drinking water fountain, but there was a pool of water at the bottom, a couple inches. From where I stood it looked clean.

I noticed that people were stopping to dab their fingers in the water and touched their forehead.

What is this, I thought??

Some people were just sticking their fingers in the water before they walked on. I followed suit, after all, I didn't want to stick out.

I walked by the long row of giant floor to ceiling windows to the right and headed for the front door of the sanctuary. As I walked, I looked out over the congregation. The room was HUGE! So many people, probably two hundred, maybe more. So many lost and hungry souls. Children crying. Organ music playing. A LOT of activity. I prayed in tongues for them, for their futures, for their families. I prayed that the air in the building would be infused with the pneuma of the Holy Spirit.

I walked into the ladies' room. A woman was in the stall next to me with one of her children. I love that. One of my favorite memories of when my children were small, and had to come into the ladies' room with me so Mommy could help. So cute.

I exited the bathroom and walked back into the main sanctuary, still praying in tongues under my breath. There was another fountain, much larger this time between the two front doors leading into the main sanctuary. I hadn't seen it on the way out, or maybe I was distracted. There was no way to avoid it this time!

Again, people dipping their fingers in, some of these people were quasi-kneeling, almost a curtsy....I was perplexed to see this.

What were they curtsying to? The water fountain?

I walked up to the fountain, and dipped my fingers in it, then walked inside the sanctuary doors to find a seat. I noticed a woman staring at me out of the corner of my eye.

Almost immediately the parade of men and women in their long robes and golden vests started, with incense and candles and a big cross-on-a-stick. Young tweens in long white robes and black tennis sneakers with tousled hair and sleep in their eyes holding up candle snuffers in front of them on long wooden sticks as they marched.

It was so formal and stilted. I watched as they circled the room, with one man swinging smoke in all directions from a giant brass ball on chains, and one man held up something huge that appeared to be an oversized book over his head as he walked. I could only assume it was the Bible, he didn't stop to explain or to show it to us.

The parade ended, and three men were seated on really fancy chairs (thrones?) in front of the room of people. A woman stood up to sing, and every time she raised her hand the choir jumped in. When she lowered her hand they stopped. Then she would sing, then raise her hand, then the choir would jump in again. It was so bizarre!

I realized that I was watching a man-made, man-thought-up regimen that probably originated before Jesus was born.

I noticed that the Lord was silent. He said nothing to me as I sat there, praying in tongues as this bizarre spectacle unfolded.

Next was a series of stand-up, sit-down, kneel and recite words from a piece of paper, all in different order. I really couldn't follow the drill, I was out of step. I watched the people around me to see what they were doing. I had no mentor here, but thankfully I had chosen a seat only a few chairs back from the very back where few could see my inexperienced ballet.

I was too busy trying to keep up with the kneeling and sitting that was going on around me to focus on the words on the piece of paper. I did recognize, however, that many people were speaking around me, but there was no emotion. It was a regimen, by rote. Not from the heart, at least from what I could see and hear.

I am certain that there were people of the faith in the room that genuinely love God. However, I saw a LOT of people that simply WERE...and a lot of them were NOT in that room. They were physically in the building, but they were elsewhere in their mind.

I kept praying.

I watched a man in a dark overcoat, dark silver hair, attractive and very well dressed. He knew all the words, all the actions. He never looked at me, but he turned in my direction several times. I suspected he was a demon. I prayed for him.

I noticed a very pretty woman with blonde hair, late thirties, with two children. She and her husband were sitting in front of me a few rows. I don't know what drew my attention to her, other than she was very pretty and she leaned over to talk to her husband several times. I dismissed them mentally, and moved my attention back to the rituals.

Next was communion. I was very nervous, as another time in Catholic Church I had been chastised by one of the people who pass out the communion elements. I knew going in that there is a specific method of taking communion in the Catholic church. One is not allowed to touch the bread (the host) and usually the wine is real.

I couldn't remember if I was supposed to dip my bread in the wine or drink from the cup or cross my arms! Thankfully when I got to the front the lady put the bread in my mouth and I walked off. No wine. I was relieved. I found out later I missed the wine guy!

I went back to my seat, the ushers passed the collection plates, there was a few songs out of the hymnal (and we sang ALL the verses!) and the priest dismissed us. The parade began again in reverse, and I left the building as quickly as I could without running.

Remembering my assignment to walk the grounds and reclaim territory for the Lord, I saw they were having a raffle for a new Toyota Tundra pickup truck in another building. It was the perfect opportunity to walk around. While I was there I just HAD to get a couple raffle tickets.

Hey, you never know!

Finally I got into my pickup truck and sat, grieving for the Holy Spirit and praying while I waited for the Mercedes and Cadillacs to clear the lot. Then I left, thankful that my first visit was over.

The second visit was less memorable, other than my husband joined me. He is far more versed in the regimen than I am. It was a lot better for me since he knew more of the stand-up-sit-down-now-kneel routine. Darryl plays his trumpet many times in denominational" churches so he has had a lot more opportunity and exposure to the routines in them.

By now I was more comfortable in doing what God asked of me. I had settled into my assignment of walking and praying to take back territory that had been stolen by the enemy.

I did see the pretty woman with her husband again this trip. I was fascinated that she was bouncing in her seat like a small child, Bobbing her feet together and unable to sit still. I hadn't noticed that the first time. I prayed that the spirit of A.D.D. (Attention Deficit Disorder) would leave her. She turned to me and smiled several times, very pleasantly, as if she recognized me, too.

My third trip to the Catholic church was amazing. God showed up, and stepped in. I supposed the field had been plowed enough for Him, or maybe it is just because it was a kairos moment. Either way, it was "time" and He showed up.

I arrived by myself at the church later than the other two times, so the seats were all starting to fill up and most of the seats in the back had already been taken. There were actually lines starting to form for seating. As I walked in, I prayed and asked the Lord where He would want me to sit. He said that he would show me.

I walked around and sat in the very back row on the same side of the church as my first visit. Two rows in front of me was a lady in a pink shirt with blonde hair that obviously had a physical handicap of some kind, but I couldn't tell exactly what kind. Next to her was a lady with her daughter, who had turned around on the bench, and kneeling on it backwards was trying to help her husband find a place to sit down. The rest of the bench was full, as was the bench directly in front of me and the place was filling up fast.

There was an empty seat next to me, but he didn't take it. There was another empty seat next to the pink shirted lady with the physical challenge, but there was no kneeling-board so no one was sitting there and he didn't take that one, either. I knew I could sit there, because I didn't need the kneeling board, and I briefly contemplated it.

Just then, Holy Spirit had me turn around and directly behind me I was surprised to see a man who was standing with his two small sons, pressed up against the wall. There was no room for three people to sit down anywhere around me.

Suddenly, the Lord moved people just like chess pieces into position.

The lady with her daughter left their seats, and now the husband didn't need a seat anymore. This development created room on the bench next to the pink lady with the physical challenge.

I decided to give my seat to the father with his two small boys. I turned to the father with his two sons that were still behind me and said, "Please, take my seat." He shook his head, but one of the other people on the row next to me moved down a little, making room for the three of them.

I got up and moved to the seat at the end of the pew with the pink lady who was physically challenged. She smiled sweetly and moved down on her pew a little. We were all in position now, and the Lord was ready for action. He was ready for Checkmate!

The service began. At the time of the meet and greet I talked to the pink lady who was now next to me. I didn't realize it at first, but in watching the pink lady move, get up and sit down, I recognized the aftermath of a stroke. It was fairly severe, and she had to lean hard on her paralyzed arm to get up and sit down, to kneel and to rise. I felt for her.

She mentioned how uncomfortable it must be for ME to kneel on the concrete floor! I laughed quietly and said it was no problem at all. What courage! And such a sweet spirit. I knew that the Lord had set me beside her to pray for her healing with her.

So, at the end of the service, before everyone was dismissed, she got up to leave. I followed her out, as during the meet and greet we had agreed to speak after the service. She led the way out of the building, and I asked her if I could pray for her. She of course said YES, everyone does.

However, few people realize that I mean RIGHT NOW, RIGHT HERE!

So, I started to pray for her, and she wept as she heard the words the Lord spoke over her, freedom from fear, freedom from trauma. She explained then that her brother had died from a stroke before she ever had hers, so the spirit of fear had set in. Once she had a stroke, the spirit of trauma jumped on her, and now she thought she was going to die like her brother! This allowed the spirit of death to come into her life, too.

Once she was free of the bondage of these spirits she felt better.

I believe that she is healed, although I have not seen her since that day. I may have to try to find her, to give her a copy of this book, so she will know how much she helped ME.

Of course, that means I would have to go back to the Catholic Church!

I heard from the Lord that day was my last time at that church, and that my assignment had been completed. He did not make me stay for a full month. I was grateful that I had completed my task there.

Whatever it was.

7 WHAT IT WAS

After a few days, following my "undercover espionage" experience, I realized that my assignment, although initially I thought was to do something for God, was actually to change something in ME.

I found through my travels and travailing that denominational churches contain PEOPLE. They may be deceived, but they are still people.

God loves people. He created them. He loves them and it is His will that NONE should perish, but that they all come to a saving knowledge of His son, Jesus.

That was the assignment. It was for me, to change my heart.

Prior to this journey, I had always looked down my nose on denominations, because the opinion I held was they were deceived, and in my estimation (read JUDGMENT) they *wanted* to be and to *stay* deceived.

It never occurred to me that they are just people, like me and you.

God had to set me free from my judgmental spirit before He could use me. Only God could come up with a plan like this!

I am sure that there are things, both attitudes and spirits, that the Lord wants YOU to be freed from, as well.

Could one be a judgmental spirit like me? A critical spirit? An unsubmissive spirit? Or a spirit of haughtiness, pride or a Jezebel spirit? A rebellious spirit? Or just not being obedient?

God loves you, and wants to activate you into your calling and ministry. He WANTS to use you. Asking Him to do that is as simple as saying, "Here am I Lord, send me!"

Then GO.

You are one of God's chess men. Get on the board!

Who knows? He may even send YOU to go undercover for the Kingdom of God!

.

ABOUT THE AUTHOR

Edie Bayer's primary focus is to promote and advance the Kingdom of God by helping people to hear and recognize the voice of the Lord, and then act upon it. Edie has served with international ministers Joan Hunter and Paulette Reed as well as Darren Canning and Dr. Judy Laird. Edie ministers as a Preacher and Prophet of God. She is an author, a speaker and itinerant minister.

Edie and her husband Darryl formed Kingdom Promoters (www.KingdomPromoters.org), to help further God's Kingdom by acting as an incubator to assist fledgling ministries in their start-up stages. Kingdom Promoters also hosts itinerant speakers and travelling ministers such as Dr. Linda Smith and Apostle William Dillon, as s well as author Carol Sewell, among others.

Edie and Darryl reside on a small homestead north of the Houston area. They raise chickens, ducks and rabbits and have two cats.

www.ingramcontent.com/pod-product-compliance
Lightning Source LLC
Chambersburg PA
CBHW071742020426
42331CB00008B/2132